Monta...
Turn...ers all...enue ...376
ls

P9-CRC-320

j593.3
Har   Hartley
             Snail

DEC 1 2 '01
  JAN 2 5 '02
AUG 0 7 '02

BUG BOOKS

Snail

Karen Hartley
and
Chris Macro

Heinemann Library
Chicago, Illinois

© 1998 Reed Educational & Professional Publishing
Published by Heinemann Library,
an imprint of Reed Educational & Professional Publishing,
Chicago, IL

Customer Service 1-888-454-2279

All rights reserved. No part of this publication may be reproduced or transmitted in any form or by
any means, electronic or mechanical, including photocopying, recording, taping, or any information
storage and retrieval system, without permission in writing from the publisher.

Designed by Celia Floyd
Illustrations by Alan Male
Printed in Hong Kong
02 01
10 9 8 7 6 5 4 3

Library of Congress Cataloging-in-Publication Data

Hartley, Karen, 1949-
    Snail / Karen Hartley and Chris Macro.
      p.   cm. -- (Bug books)
    Includes bibliographical references and index.
    Summary: A simple introduction to the physical characteristics,
diet, life cycle, predators, habitat, and lifespan of snails.
    ISBN 1-57572-664-5 (lib. bdg.)
    1. Snails--Juvenile literature. [1. Snails.] I. Macro, Chris,
1940-. II. Title. III. Series.
QL430.4.H346 1998
593'.3--dc21   98-4857
                                          CIP
                                          AC

Paperback ISBN 1-57572-460-X

Acknowledgments
The Publishers would like to thank the following for permission to reproduce photographs: Ardea
London: pp.14, 26, J. Daniels p. 8, J. Mason p. 13, P. Morris p. 4; Bruce Coleman: J. Burton pp. 24, 25,
W. Layer p. 23, H. Reinhard p. 15, K. Taylor pp. 11, 16, 18; FLPA: A. Wharton p. 20; Chris Honeywell
pp. 28, 29; Nature Photographers: P. Sterry p. 12; NHPA: M. Tweedie p. 10; Oxford Scientific Films:
G. Bernard p. 27; M. Birkhead p. 9, L. Crowhurst p. 7, W. Gray p. 19, J. Pontier p. 5, T. Tilford p. 22;
Planet Earth Pictures:S. Hopkins pp. 6, 21; Premaphotos: K. Preston-Mafham p. 17

Cover photograph reproduced with permission of child: Chris Honeywell; snail: M. Mattock/Telegraph
Color Library

Every effort has been made to contact copyright holders of any material reproduced in this book. Any
omissions will be rectified in subsequent printings if notice is given to the Publisher.

Any words appearing in the text in bold, **like this**, are explained in the Glossary.

Contents

What are snails?

Snails have a soft body and carry a hard shell. They do not have any legs. Some snails live in water but in this book we will be looking at snails that live in gardens and woods.

Snails come in different sizes and have shells of different colors. Some snails are very small. Some are very big. This is a Giant African land snail. It can grow to be longer than your foot!

What do snails look like?

Snails have a thick, soft **foot** that they can pull into their hard shell. Each ring on the shell is called a **whorl**. The soft foot usually feels damp and slimy.

Snails have a mouth under their head and a breathing hole under their shell. The short **antennae** are used for touch and smell. The long ones have two tiny eyes at the end.

How big are snails?

Adult garden snails are about as long as one of your middle fingers when they are moving. Baby snails are about the size of your little fingernail.

Snails are much smaller when they are inside their shells. As snails grow, their shells get bigger.

How are snails born?

Snails make a hole in the soil and lay eggs there. They usually lay about 40 eggs at a time. The eggs are white.

After about 21 days, the eggs **hatch** and the baby snails begin to move around. They have little shells and very **pale** bodies.

How do snails grow?

The snail's body gets darker as it gets older. In the first year the shell has about three **whorls**. Can you see them?

The snail is fully grown when it is about two years old. It will have about five whorls on its shell.

What do snails eat?

Snails like to eat dead leaves or plants which are brown and smelly. If there are no dead leaves then snails will eat fresh, green plants.

Sometimes snails eat the green **algae** off the branches of trees. Some snails will even eat other snails but they would rather eat plants.

Which animals attack snails?

Snails' predators usually attack at night. Rats, large beetles, and ducks like to eat snails. Some birds break open the snail's shell on stones and then peck at the soft body.

When a snail senses it is in danger, it will hide in its shell. Sometimes it makes **froth** come out from under the shell to scare off its attackers.

Where do snails live?

Many snails live in gardens. They also live in woods, bushes, and grass. They like damp, dark places.

You can often find snails under stones. After it has been raining you may see them climbing up walls. Snails can cling very tightly to walls and stones.

How do snails move?

Snails move slowly. They move more quickly when it is warm and wet. The muscles in the **foot** make the snail move. Can you see the muscles in this foot?

Snails make slime to help them to slide over bumpy paths and stones. They make more slime when they are going uphill or are on bumpy ground.

How long do snails live?

If snails live where there are many predators, they do not live for very long. Can you see the empty shells? The snails have been eaten.

Some garden snails can live for five years. Some **desert** snails can stay in their shells for years, without eating or moving. They live much longer than busy garden snails.

Montague Public Libraries
201 Avenue A
Turners Falls, MA 01376

What do snails do?

Snails come out when the weather is damp. When the weather is very hot snails stop eating and bury themselves. Snails will also hide if the weather is very cold.

Snails mostly look for food at night. It is safer in the dark.

How are snails special?

Snails can smell strong smells through their **antennae**. If a snail smells something it does not like, it goes into its shell. Sometimes snails like to stay very close together.

When snails **hibernate** for the winter, or when it is hot, they make a skin over the opening of the shell. This is called the **epiphragm** (EH-peh-fram).

Thinking about Snails

Which food do you think the snail will like best? What are the snails' **antennae** used for?

Which surface do you think the snail likes best? Will the snail make more slime when it is moving on the carpet or on the smooth wood?

What would make it easier to move?

Snail Map

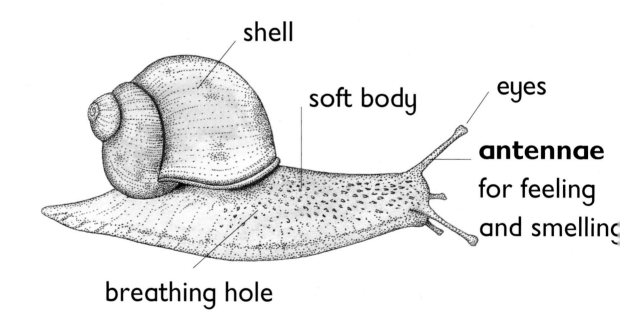

shell

soft body

eyes

antennae
for feeling
and smelling

breathing hole

Glossary

algae a green slime that grows on the branches and trunks of trees

antenna (More than one are called **antennae**) long thin tubes on a snail's head. These are used for feeling and smelling. The eyes are at the end of the **antennae**.

desert bare land that has little or no rain

epiphragm the skin that the snail makes to cover the opening of its shell

foot the soft body of the snail that comes out of the shell

froth white foam a snail makes when it is in danger. It comes out from under the shell.

hatch to be born out of an egg

pale light in color, almost white

whorls the rings on a snail's shell

More Books to Read

Oleson, Jens. *Snail*. Columbus, Oh.: Silver Press, 1986.
Watts, Barrie. *Slugs & Snails*. Danbury, Conn.:
Watts, 1991.

Index